J

By the same author

TOO RISKY!
TOO FRISKY!

JIM DAVIDSON'S TRUE BRIT

Jim Davidson & Neil Shand

ARROW

Arrow Books Limited
20 Vauxhall Bridge Road, London SW1V 2SA

An imprint of the Random Century Group

London Melbourne Sydney Auckland
Johannesburg and agencies throughout
the world

First published by Robson Books Ltd in 1991

This edition published in 1992 by Arrow Books

1 3 5 7 9 10 8 6 4 2

ILLUSTRATED BY
JIM HUTCHINGS

Printed and bound in Great Britain by
Cox & Wyman Ltd., Reading, Berkshire

ISBN 0 09 919131 8

FOREWORD

I've always thought that the further you get away from Kidbrooke SE23, the thicker people become. And I don't say that just because I was born there (they'll be putting the little blue plaque up any day now, though what's the betting Mary Whitehouse complains that it's too blue, without even seeing it?).

No, I happen to think it's true about Kidbrooke SE23 – which is next door to Charlton Nil, as it's known on the sports programmes – and the rest of the world. Especially that bit of the world across the Channel. That's the ENGLISH Channel, by the way. I mean, look at the Spanish. How could a country like that get an Armada together? Who else would let in all of London's underworld? No wonder we keep a military presence in Gibraltar. And as for the French, I can't see the point of them. All a waste of garlic. And if they don't want our lamb then quite frankly I don't want their letters.

We've been making jokes about the Continentals for centuries and they've probably been making jokes about us. But as they couldn't be bothered to tell them in English how would we know? It's all harmless fun really. Just our lovable British way of reminding them – in the absence of the odd war, a recent Eurovision victory or a few more World Cups like the one in '66 – that we're still superior, still Number One.

Now all this could be about to change. At the end of 1992 Europe becomes a single market (don't ask), taking us closer to that day when Europe becomes like one country, when our European cousins become our European brothers and some Europrat in Brussels will point the finger – probably the same finger he pointed at our cigarette ads, our crisps and our beer – and say NO MORE EUROJOKES.

This book is written in anticipation of that terrible day, a last chance to 'prenez le Perrier'.

Hope you enjoy it, and if we've offended anyone I would just like to say in all sincerity - BALLEAUX.

A IS FOR ABSINTHE. A potent drink made largely from wormwood. Reputed to be an aphrodisiac, as in 'Absinthe makes the part grow fonder.'

★

A is also for **AIRPORT.** Continental airports are different from British airports. In most cases they've finished building them. Except for Athens where they never started.

★

A is also for **AIR TRAFFIC CONTROLLERS** also known as 'those French/Spanish bastards'. A number of times every year European air traffic controllers decide to work to rule. The rule is that the British shouldn't be allowed to fly anywhere. They always wait until that moment when you're waving goodbye to your loved ones, wondering whether you'll ever see them again, (we're of course talking about your luggage) before announcing it. Your flight can then be delayed until Hell freezes over or until somebody comes to clear away the dirty cups and empty the ashtrays in the departure lounge, whichever is the sooner.

But flight delays can be useful. Why not wander round the departure area picking up things for the trip, like a Swedish air hostess? Or an Italian purser? Whatever turns you on. You can also spend many happy hours in the duty free shop, buying gallons of export strength Scotch, cartons of cigarettes and jumbo size flasks of His Thing, the new industrial-strength Body Rub from Brute. It's fortified with the undiluted essence of the genital glands of the musk-ox, the most powerful sexual attractant in the animal kingdom. Women hate it, but if you ever run into a musk-ox you'll have a night you'll never forget.

It's always a good idea to consume at least half of your duty free booze on the journey so that by the time you check into your hotel you're well and truly rat-arsed and in precisely the right frame of mind to slag off the receptionist (if your room isn't ready), throw up in the potted palm and generally leave them in no doubt at all as to who you are, and what you are. Incidentally, if you find Spanish and Greek waiters and hotel workers telling you to 'get stuffed' don't take it per-

'Did you hear that, Maurice? Dreadful man just told me to get stuffed!'

sonally. Over the years they've been told to 'get stuffed' on so many different occasions, by so many different Brits, that they now think it's an all-purpose English expression meaning 'Good morning/Good evening/Thank you/Don't mention it and I think your country's wonderful.'

★

A is also for ALSACE, the region of France where the people and not the dogs are called Alsatians. So don't wander round Alsace telling the locals, 'Never turn your back on an Alsatian, you never know when they'll go for you.' They call Alsatians German shepherds. Doesn't sound right, does it? We can't hear some hairy skip driver from Essex saying to his mates, 'The wife wants a German shepherd to keep her company in the evenings. I think I'll give her one.' Besides, you know what sheep say, 'Never turn your back on a German shepherd, especially if he's wearing flying boots.'

★

A is also for AMSTERDAM, which is where Max Bygraves got the tulips and very lucky he was when you consider some of the things you can get there. Amsterdam has a famous red light district where the working girls display themselves in windows, looking not unlike those naked dummies in Oxford Street department stores before the window dressers get to work. The only difference between the two is that the dummies have better figures and are a lot more animated. It should be said that these ladies are not exactly Holland's answer to Kim Bassinger or Julia Roberts but that's still no reason for window shoppers to walk past singing 'How much is that doggie in the window?' Even if she does have a wiggly tail. These establishments usually take credit cards so if you have a flexible friend, don't leave home without it.

Amsterdam is also one of the world's movie capitals. Who can forget such great classics as *Meter Maids on the Job, Debbie's Double Dutch Treat,* and *Helga and Her Farmyard Friends,* for which Helga was given a special lifetime achievement award by the World Wildlife Fund for 'reaching those parts that David Attenborough never reached.'

Amsterdam is not, however, a city of fine restaurants: *Famous Dutch Chefs* is one of the thinnest books in the world. One of the most popular dishes is Erwtensoep which is easier to eat than it is to say. It's pea soup, which you can get almost anywhere except at the headquarters of Amstel and Heineken. You work it out.

A is for **AUSTRIA** which is not yet in the Common Market but which soon will be. In anticipation of that eagerly awaited day – there'll certainly be a party in our street – *here are ten things you must never say to an Austrian:*

Got any white wine? My radiator's leaking.

You're really Germans, aren't you?

You wouldn't get me sharing a shower with a bloke who likes dressing up in little leather shorts and slapping himself.

Wasn't Hitler an Austrian?

Wolfgang Amadeus who?

Remember me to Mr Waldheim.

Of course I've heard of Freud. Pedigree Chum.

What did you do in the war?

What's the Austrian for 'smug, self satisfied berk'?

I know Schubert lived here, but let's face it, he's no Andrew Lloyd Webber, is he?

The Austrians do a lot of walking and now their northern neighbour is happily reunified they could be doing a lot more in the not too distant future.

Austria exports thousands of Tyrolean hats to Australia. Women are very partial to a long curly feather down under.

B IS FOR BARDOT, Brigitte Bardot, who cleared up more teenage pimples than Valderma. She had legs like one of Neil Kinnock's speeches; they went on for ever. Whenever she appeared in St-Tropez in a bikini every man gave her a standing ovation. Today she devotes her life to saving the animals. If that's a success she'll move on and try to save the Kinks and Freddie and the Dreamers.

★

B is also for **BASQUE,** the home of the Basque Separatists, the revolutionary group who seek independence for the Basque country, which was the location of one of the great disasters of recent times when nine hundred people perished trying to escape through the only door of a blazing cinema. The proprietor was accused by the police of putting all his Basques into one exit. Basque is also the name of an exotic item of ladies' lingerie and what it separates certainly aren't tists.

***B is also for* BAVARIA** in southern Germany. Actually, it's the deep south. When they greet each other they say 'Guten morgen you-all.' Bavaria is the traditional home of German nationalism. In Bavaria the geese march about the place doing the people-step. The service in the restaurants and bars is excellent, nobody has any problem taking orders. The pubs are not called pubs but bierkellers where World War II veterans entertain up-and-coming young Nazis with the baring of shrapnel scars, whilst singing countless choruses of the 'Horst Wessel', the German equivalent of ''Ere We Go, 'Ere We Go, 'Ere We Go', and whingeing about how different things would have been if the Führer hadn't wimped out. While they're doing all this they consume vast quantities of Bavarian beer, the beer that invades the parts other beers can't march on, in huge mugs called steins. Incidentally, Bavarian steins are different from Australian steins, which are usually found down the front of an ocker's trousers.

When he discovers you are a Brit, your average Bavarian, who can make a tattooed pit-bull breeder from Forest Gate seem about as threatening as a camp florist, will stop scuffing his knuckles on the ground and start to taunt you about England's football record. They will shout things like 'Ve beat you at your national game, Tommy.' When they do, quote them the words of that wise Brit who said, 'And we beat you at yours. Twice.' Or, in the words of Field-Marshal Montgomery, 'Played two, won two.'

★

B is also for **BELGIUM AND BELGIANS.**
Here are ten things you should never say to a Belgian:

Who's Eddie Merkx?

Excuse me, am I still in Belgium or did I miss it?

Name five famous Belgians.

I prefer Cadbury's.

You must have been delighted when the Germans got back together again.

Is there such a thing as a Belgian comedian?

Some of my best friends are Walloons.

What's the Belgian for 'dickhead'?

You don't look like an arms dealer.

Your chips are crap.

The national dish of Belgium is chips, which is why so many of the European food mountains are actually Belgians. The most famous sight in Belgium is the statue of the little boy peeing into the fountain. Actually, he's not peeing into the fountain at all, he's putting the bubbles into the mineral water they flog us. The Belgians speak Flemish and frequently sound it, but as they are the only people who do, don't bother to learn it.

★

B is also for **BERLIN,** once again the capital of a united Germany, and soon, some fear, to be the capital of a united Europe. Nobody dare say 'over my dead body' because that never stopped anybody before. The most exciting prospect about the new Berlin is that she could once again become the naughtiest city in Europe. Berlin in the thirties, they tell us, makes present-day Amsterdam look about as sinful as Tamworth on a wet Tuesday in October.

Perhaps we shall see a return to the telephone bars, where every table had its telephone and if you saw somebody you fancied you dialled their table. And if you got a heavy breather at least you could see what they looked like before you hung up. And, of course, it cut out all that boring 'tell me what you've got on' business. Some enterprising young businessman tried to open a telephone bar in Glasgow when the city was the Cultural Capital of Europe (all that meant was you got mugged in French by Glaswegian dwarfs shouting 'see vous, Jimmy') but it was a failure because all the callers tried to reverse the charges. The Berlin telephone bar is believed to be the first instance of telephone sex, the phenomenon which must be contributing at least half of the twenty billion pounds' profit British Telecom has made in the time it's taken you to read this sentence. It's become so popular you can hear guys in the pubs boasting 'I bet my bill's bigger than yours.'

Berlin in the thirties catered to every sexual peccadillo known to man, plus a few that weren't. You couldn't be sure whether a Herr was a her or a she was a he and whether you were into bondage, sandpaper, warm custard or merely liked tadpoles down your trousers – thirties Berlin could lay it on.

The German President, Herr Kohl – he can't get anybody to take him and his wife to Newcastle – reckons it will take ten years to restore Berlin to its former glory. Perhaps, for a change, the EC could do something to brighten our lives, and urge them to get a move on.

★

B is also for **BIDET.** It's essential that you know the difference between a duvet and a bidet. Failure in this has led to some nasty accidents when British travellers, surprised by a sudden drop in the temperature, have insisted on their hotels throwing another bidet on the bed. Similarly, there have been embarrassing scenes when Brits have complained about the little squirt on the duvet in the bathroom. The duvet is that soft, lumpy thing you throw on the bed unless your partner is in Weightwatchers, in which case it's the soft, lumpy thing you throw over the soft, lumpy thing that's already on the bed. Continental duvets are usually stuffed with down and are ideal for people who like a little goose in the night. The bidet is the low-level footbath usually located between the washbasin and the WC, or, as they call it in France, the water loo. One English lady, on encountering her first bidet, said to the hotel manager: 'Ah, and I suppose this is for washing the baby in!' 'Non madam,' said the manager. 'That is for washing ze baby out.'

★

B is also for **BOIS DE BOULOGNE,** an area of Paris where boys will be boys, even if most of them prefer

'*Monsieur ordered an extra bidet, yes?*'

dressing up as girls. If that's your penchant, or, if you're over sixty-five, your old age penchant, then it might be worth dragging yourself along.

★

B is also for **BOULES,** a game played by Frenchmen who gather together in an open space to see who can throw their boules the furthest. It can bring tears to the eyes.

★

B is also for **BRUSSELS,** home of the people who run the Common Market, the Eurocrats, or, as they're fondly known as, the Europrats. Thus far, the EPs have said we shouldn't call our chocolate chocolate because there's not enough chocolate in it, they say our beer hasn't got enough beer in it, and we're still waiting for a ruling on spotted dick. R and R used to mean rest and recreation; in Brussels it stands for rules and regulations. And just about the only certainty in these uncertain times is that there are going to be zillions of lovely new rules and regulations to clog up our lives. Sting can stop worrying about the rain forests. At the rate that Brussels will soon be consuming paper there won't be a tree left in the world.

★

B is also for **BULLFIGHTING.** This used to be the national sport of Spain before the Spaniards discovered a) football and b) female British holidaymakers. At a bullfight the matador attracts the bull by making a pass at it with his cape (Spaniards will make a pass at anything). If the matador makes a successful pass the correct response is to shout 'Olé!' and not 'By 'eck I bet there's a few Oxo cubes in that bugger.' If the bullfighter is very good he is awarded the bull's ears. If he's very bad the bull gets his pick. There are now a number of British bullfighters in Spain and it's easy to pick them out – they're the ones in the anoraks and brown trousers.

C IS FOR CALAIS which was forever etched upon the heart of Mary Tudor. Calais was also the point beyond which the water was not even considered safe enough to wash socks in. Nowadays nobody need worry about the water – the hypermarkets have got shelves groaning with the stuff. And as for washing socks, Evian's perfectly safe.

Some people will get their first taste of driving on the right-hand side of the road when they roll off the car ferry at Calais. This can be nerve-racking, as the local yobs know. They hang around looking for a bright new GB sticker and then terrorize driver and passengers. If this happens to you, don't get mad, get even. When you're back in Britain make your way to Park Lane in London where many French holiday coaches park. Because they are now on the wrong side of the road these buses disgorge their French passengers into

the streams of oncoming British traffic. We think you know what you have to do.

C is also for **CHANNEL TUNNEL,** which many believe will lead to a serious outbreak of rabbis in southern England in 1993. When the Channel Tunnel finally opens Britain will technically no longer be an island and millions of Eurobeings will swarm through the tunnel in special shoppers' trains and descend like locusts upon every Marks & Spencer in the land. It will be like one of those plagues in the Old Testament:

And lo it was written that there was a promised land where the knickers were abundant and where the Y-fronts were bounteous and where the storerooms bulged with men's V-neck sweaters and ladies' leisure pants, yea, even unto the size XXL. And in a land across the water there lived a motley tribe called the Eurobeings who had heard talk of this land of socks and knickers and they did journey unto it and waited for the seas to part but the High Priests said that that had been done, why not build a tunnel. And so it came to pass after forty years and forty knighthoods that a great tunnel was builded and the Eurobeings poured forth from it, a great garlic smelling multitude who descended upon the knickers and the socks and the Thai recipe dishes to be frozen on the day of purchase and eaten within ONE MONTH, and in the words of Abraham, they copped the lot. And the Lord (Sieff) was mighteous pleased. But the people were exceeding angry and they told the Eurobeings to go forth and multiply themselves.

That's how it will be – at sale time the Eurohordes will move in so fast that not even the staff will have a chance to cream off the best of the bargains. All they will leave behind will be empty shelves and rails, underpants that would look big on Cyril Smith, bras that Dolly Parton could share with a friend and any drip-dry white shirt with brown stripes and a matching Terylene tie costing less than £7.99.

In addition to becoming the boutique of Europe – what was that Napoleon said about a nation of shopkeepers? – there's also a rumour that the Disney people are thinking of buying Britain, closing it down and reopening it as Fergieland, a Royal theme park, where

Prince Philip will give coach rides, where Prince Charles and Princess Diana will go on *Blind Date* in a final effort to meet one another and where Prince Edward will organize a non-stop version of *It's A Royal Cock Up*. Nobody is yet certain what the Queen will do but most think it won't be very taxing. Fergieland won't bear any resemblance to the Britain we know. It will be a total fantasy. For starters, all the motorways will be free of roadworks. Our only hope is that the Tunnel somehow gets blocked. Maybe they could award the cleaning contract to Liverpool Public Cleansing Department.

***C is also for* SENORINA CICCIOLINA,** the Italian stripper and blue movie star who is now an Italian MP and the subject of more party whip jokes than the erstwhile tenant of Norman Lamont's basement. She takes her parliamentary duties very seriously and is really getting down to it on the back benches. But she still hangs out with old friends. They call her the Edwina Currie of Italy, though of course Mrs Currie is famous for opening her mouth.

***C is also for* COJONES,** which the Eurocrats in Brussels frequently speak a load of. (It's OK, in Europe everybody ends their sentences with a proposition.)

***C is also for* COMPOSERS.** Europe has a lot of compo-

sers, though most of them are now decomposers. The
only two the Brits are really interested in are Brahms
and Liszt.

★

C is also for **CONDOM,** which in addition to being
essential baggage also happens to be the name of a
region of France. We talk of sending coals to Newcastle, the French speak of sending letters to Condom. We
call a condom a French letter, the French call it an
English hat, a *capot anglais*. Typical. Which English
hat is it supposed to be? A bowler, a pork pie, a silk
topper, a deerstalker, an Anthony Eden? Could make
a difference. Actually it's probably a hard hat.

In Ireland the only place you can buy condoms is in
a Virgin shop. And they complain about Irish jokes.
But it's also possible to get condoms on prescription in
Ireland. Imagine standing in the doctor's waiting room
and being told by his nurse, 'Only keep you a moment,
the doctor's just filling out your prescription now.'

Here's a fascinating statistic: the average Russian
male buys twelve condoms a year. From Russia With
Love, but not very often. The alternative doesn't bear
thinking about. But it should be remembered that until
recently the Russians didn't need condoms, they prac-
tised a unique form of birth control, KGB-interruptus.
There's a wonderful story told about Russia and
condoms during World War II. In 1943, with her war
machine taking up every ounce of rubber, Russia was
running out of condoms. With the nation's barbers
unable to offer anything for the weekend Stalin con-
tacted the British Prime Minister, Winston Churchill,
and asked for help. Winston is supposed to have called

in the chairman of the London Rubber Company and asked him to send a hundred thousand of his biggest condoms to Russia with the following printed on each of them: 'Made in England, Medium'.

★

***C is also for* CRESSON.** Mme Edith Cresson is the French Prime Minister who thinks British men are about as sexy as window putty. She also thinks that one in four of them is gay. Which, if it's true, means that if you're in a pub with three of your mates and none of them is gay then it's got to be you. 'Frenchmen are much more interested in women,' said Mme 'Mornington' Cresson. 'Anglo-Saxon men are not. In Paris a workman, or indeed any man, looks at passing women. I remember from strolling about in London that the men in the streets don't look at you.' Where was Mme Cresson strolling? The Dominican Priory in Hampstead? Or the People's Republic of Islington where it's now an offence for a man to look at a woman or an 'unappendaged gender unit', as they call them? It certainly wasn't in the West End, or the City or Docklands, where the streets echo with the mating calls of the Great Horned British Scaffolder: "Allo darlin'. Get 'em off. Bleedin' 'ell, Wayne, look at the knockers on that. Come up 'ere, darlin', I couldn't 'alf give you a good seeing to.' Put a dog in a skirt and those lads would give it the treatment, indeed they frequently do.

How then to answer Mme Cresson's scurrilous accusation? It's no good turning to the government. When the Foreign Office were asked for their view, they said the Minister was tied up and they weren't prepared to reveal his position. Perhaps the Nicholas Ridley Foundation for Anglo-European Friendship could sponsor MachoBrit, an organization that could arrange cheap trips to Paris for scaffolders, van drivers, removal men and window cleaners who could stroll the streets of the city not just looking at passing women, like any boring old French fart, but telling them what they thought as well: 'Bleedin' merde, Wayne, regardez les knockers sur ça. Ascendez ici, darlin', je voudrai vous donner un bon seeing to.' And just to ram the message home, so to speak, they'll wear T-shirts with the message 'How about a Brit'. Incidentally, Mme 'Water' Cresson also thinks that twenty-five per cent of all Germans are gay, so the next time you go down to the pool in your Spanish hotel to find a towel already on your favourite sunbed, check the colour. If it's pink, you could be on a promise.

★

C is also for **CRICKET.** One reason why so many people have been against closer ties with Europe is that Euro-folk don't play cricket. They probably think something with three slips, a silly short leg and a backward point is one of Mme Cresson's twenty-five per cent.

★

C is also for **CRIME PASSIONELLE** which more or less means that if you decide to bump off your spouse because he/she/it talks through *Match of the Day,* squeezes the toothpaste in the wrong place, does unspeakable things with a salami and a Black and

Decker under the shower or unreasonably insists on sex at least seven times a year, in France it would probably be treated as a crime of passion and you could expect, at the very most, to get only a light sentence and possibly freedom. So clearly, if you are feeling a bit iffy about him/her/it, there's no point in hanging around in the Home Counties, nipping down to the local DIY for a chainsaw (The Texas Homecare Massacre), doing the deed and end up getting life. Hop on a hovercraft, nip over to France and do it there. We're not saying you'll get off *'écosse* free' but at least the food is better in your average French nique and of course there's always the duty frees to be picked up on the way home when they let you out.

C is also for **CROISSANT.** Many Brits wonder whether it's OK to copy the French and dunk their breakfast croissant in their coffee. Of course it is, but not if you're drinking your coffee out of the saucer.

D IS FOR DE GAULLE, the French leader who was named after a Paris airport. Britain would have been in Europe in 1963 if de Gaulle (which is French for 'that miserable old sod') hadn't said *Non*. De Gaulle was amazingly tall and it's thought that his dislike of the British dated from World War II when he was based here as leader of the Free French – we're talking liberty here not hospitality – and we kept putting him up in beds that were too short and then spread the rumour that he'd got cold feet. One way or another we got up his nose – Lord knows there was room enough.

★

***D is also for* DELORS,** the *Sun*'s favourite European. Jacques Delors is the President of the European Commission who explained the idea of a Federal Europe in

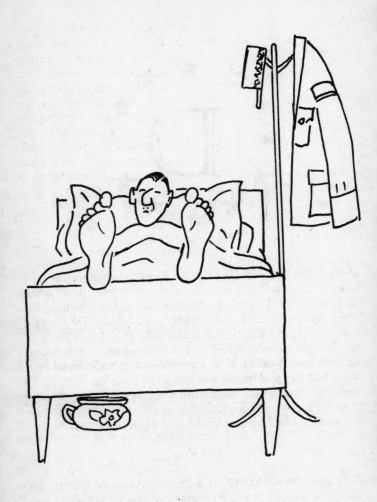

the following words: 'Federalism is a system of co-ordination of autonomous activities of a number of entities. These entities then decide to create a structure above them to which they delegate certain powers. This respects the diversity of each entity and also brings the citizen closer to the source of the power,' thereby winning outright the Neil Kinnock Award for Brevity. No wonder Mrs Thatcher used to belt him with her handbag, laying down Delors, as it were. Delors used to call her mother-figure, or something like that. Whether we like it or not we're going to hear a lot more from M. Delors.

D is also for DENMARK.
Ten things you should never say to a Dane:

You can't beat the taste of New Zealand butter.

If Shakespeare hadn't written *Hamlet* nobody would ever have heard of you.

If it hadn't been for Victor Borge nobody would ever have heard of you.

If it hadn't been for Nina and Frederick nobody would ever have heard of you.

I think you'll find scientists have discovered that bacon causes cancer.

Got any English pastries?

Is it true what they say about Danish men?

What's the Danish for 'where can I get a valium'?

Got any cheddar?

Cheer up.

In the sixties when most young Brits were still getting over the discovery that when a girl took her clothes off she didn't have a striped beach ball between her legs, Denmark's porn-again Kristians were showing the world that Danish blue wasn't necessarily a cheese, and inspiring the question: If masturbation stunts your growth why are all the porno mags on the top shelf? The combination of boredom – been there, seen that, got the Polaroids – and failing eyesight led to a shrinking of the Danish porn industry and despite intense activity from the porn workers' union, the TGWU (Tittilation and Genital Workers), including a telethon on Danish TV (Hand Relief) on which everybody was asked to wear a red condom, these days most people seem to end up banging Olufsen.

★

D is also for DISNEYWORLD, the European branch of which opens in France in 1992 with special European attractions like The Magic Food Mountain, The French Revolution, complete with working guillotine (late night chopping, Fridays) and a re-creation of World War II which will be run backwards twice a day to give German visitors a happy ending. Nobody knows yet whether Disneyworld will apply for full membership of the Common Market but we think they should. Then they can find out what it's like to live in a real Mickey Mouse world.

★

D is also for **DUVET** (see Bidet).

E IS FOR EMS, the European Monetary System; ERM, the Exchange Rate Mechanism; and ECU, the European Currency Unit. It is dangerous to drive or operate heavy machinery after reading an explanation of any or all of the above. They are part of a grand plan, culminating presumably in a single European currency. No more pounds, no more lire, no more francs, no more going to the bank to pick up foreign currency and no more wondering why you get so few francs for your pound going out and so few pounds for your francs coming back.

But come the glorious day when the cash registers of Europe resound to the clatter of the new single currency, what will it be called? It can't be ecu. That sounds like something women get on their feet. It'll take some sorting and we wouldn't be surprised if some genius in Brussels doesn't say, 'Tell you what, while all this is going on, why don't the British take their share of our wonderful new single European currency and, just for the moment, mind, call it pounds, and the French, they can take their share and call it francs and ....' In the meantime people ask what is the difference between a soft ECU and a hard ECU. The soft ECU has had too much to drink. (NB. Nobody knows whose head will adorn the new currency. The Gnomes of Zurich and the Boys in the Bund are said to favour Ken Dodd.)

E is also for **ENTENTE CORDIALE,** which is not a soft drink, but the term traditionally used to describe the special friendship between Britain and France. That's why you don't hear it much these days.

E is also for **ESCARGOT.** Pronounced to rhyme with Wells Fargo, escargots are snails. Never ask for 'escargotts' or French waiters will do something disgusting in your soup. Cooked in butter and garlic they are delicious but don't eat the shells. The French like to load them with high explosive and sell them to Iraq and Argentina.

E is also for **EUROPE** which is what this book is all about. After 1992 Europe will be a single market, more or less, which will mean that you can be unemployed in twelve countries at once. Lobby your Euro MP

'Ve have vays of making you valk!'

immediately about collecting twelve Giros. After 1992 when you want to borrow a few thousand for a new kitchen, a new garden patio or a hitman you won't have to trot along to the Listening Bank and hope that somebody is – now you can go to the First Bacon of Denmark or the Vatican's favourite bank, the Banco Ambrosiana, though they have a reputation for keeping people hanging around, especially on bridging loans. Local authorities will be able to ask anybody in the twelve countries to work for them, so as well as

French dustmen and Danish school teachers, we could have German traffic wardens, Dutch lollipop ladies in their distinctive caps, and Italian bus drivers. We'd still get six buses arriving all at once – but now they would be abreast.

★

***E is also for* EUROSPEAK,** which is itself Eurospeak for cobbblers (see Cojones). There's going to be a lot of this, the trick is to understand what the speaker's really saying:

Germany is not interested in dominating Europe.
(*It's the world we're after.*)

The member countries want Britain to take her proper place in Europe.
(*Somewhere behind Albania, San Marino and Crete.*)

We want Britain to have a proper say in European affairs.
(*This is what we want her to say.*)

The New Europe will speak with one voice.
(*It will have a German accent.*)

EC Regulation B 312/X/SW81BT governing the size and consistency of selected tubers subjected to an oil-based heat process and multiple flavouring enhancements comes into effect on 1 January 1993.
(*There go the crisps.*)

Estate agents will be naturals at Eurospeak.

E is also for **EUROVISION SONG CONTEST,** the competition for people who don't like music. It is reckoned that the last Eurovision Song Contest was watched on more than five hundred million television sets around the world – two hundred million in Europe, two hundred million in North Africa and South America and one hundred million in North America. Nobody bothered to watch in Japan, they were too busy making television sets. The Eurovision Song Contest has nothing to do with the Common Market. It is very successful. EC plans to launch a Eurovision Joke Contest had to be abandoned when nine of the countries didn't know what a joke was and the other three could only think of Jacques Delors. The trouble with European jokes is that most of them work in Brussels.

E is also for **EXOCET,** the mother of missiles. (The authors are using the term 'mother' in the Saddam Hussein sense and not the Black American.) The French appear to have sold Exocets to most of the unstable countries of the world. Most people call this madness, the French call it business. Exocets can be unreliable, indeed the only certain thing about the ones they've sold is that sooner or later they'll be fired at the British.

F IS FOR FANFANI, who used to be the Prime Minister of Italy. But then, who didn't? In Europe prime ministers come and go, except in Italy where they just go.

F is also for FERRARI, the most desirable car in the world and the ultimate tart trap. Popular with rich Italians, indeed rich anything, who use their Ferraris to pull the world's most beautiful young women. They certainly don't use them to pull caravans.

★

F is also for FOOD MOUNTAINS. Not a great deal has been heard about these since Prince Philip visited the beef mountain and said it was all bullocks. These mountains are made of surplus food that Common Market farmers are paid to produce to feed people who have more than enough to eat already. But don't tell them that in Ethiopia.

F is also for **FOOTBALL,** the game we taught the world to play. They play the game differently on the Continent where they still like to kick the ball around, unlike this country where we like to kick the manager around.

F is also for **FOREIGN LANGUAGES.** There are a lot of these in Europe and sometimes the natives can be real shits and insist on speaking in theirs. If this happens to you, do what Brits have been doing for centuries. Speak very slowly and very loudly and when the Euro-dummy still fails to understand, turn to your companion and say, 'You see, I told you, they're all bloody idiots.' This won't help you to find out what you want to know but it will make you feel superior which, after all, is the position most Brits assume naturally when they are in another country. In most European countries English is now taught as a second language, as indeed it is in many parts of Britain.

F is also for **FRANCE.**
Ten things never to say to a Frenchman:

De Gaulle was a wanker.

They've got one of those in Blackpool.

What's the Argentinian for Exocet?

Could I have a bottle of Australian red?

They say Joan of Arc was hot stuff.

Any Beef Wellington?

Why don't French Impressionists do Maurice Chevalier?

I think your lot are funnier in *'Allo, 'Allo*.

What's the French for 'untrustworthy bastard'?

Could I have my steak well done?

F is also for **FRASCATI,** an Italian white wine whose vintages are measured in weeks rather than years. In its rougher varieties Frascati makes a perfectly adequate paint stripper. It goes very well with cheap Italian food but then so does Alka Seltzer.

★

F is also for **FRENCH,** as in French kiss. Nobody knows for certain who invented the French kiss. Some believe it was a monk in the Middle Ages who had the gift of tongues, while others believe it was the famous eighteenth century glutton, Ruy de Vaux who after dinner one night noticed that his mistress still had a sizeable chunk of roast venison parked behind one of her molars and decided to go after it.

'If that's all you're after, you'd better help yourself!'

F is also for FRENCH DRESSING, FRENCH LEAVE AND FRENCH POLISHING, the meaning of which varies according to whether you're in a restaurant, a furniture restorers or a massage parlour.

F is also for FRENCH FARMERS who set fire to lorryloads of English lamb and then say: 'We thought ze

English always liked zair meat burnt.' In a typical French gesture the petrol was garlic flavoured.

★

F is also for **FRENCH KNICKERS** an item of women's sexy underwear which most men can't wait to take off. Why they were wearing French knickers in the first place is none of our business.

★

F is also for **FRENCH LETTER** (see Condom).

★

F is also for **FRENCH TICKLER,** the condom that's guaranteed to tease. The authors understand that the 'ultimate sensitivity' of the basic item is enhanced by the strategic addition of a bird's feather and though they don't know which bird the feather comes from they think a duck is out of the question.

★

F is also for **FRENCH VERMOUTH,** without which one of the greatest pleasures of civilization, the perfect dry Martini, would not be possible. To make, take a bottle of French vermouth and photograph it. Pour four fingers of Bombay gin over ice and shake well. Show the gin the photograph of the vermouth, then pour into a chilled glass. Add an olive and a twist. Perfection.

F is also for **FROGS' LEGS,** which are very popular in France especially in restaurants where the customers like to table hop. Nobody knows who first caught a frog and ate the legs; his identity is lost in the mists of thyme but it was all part of that fine French tradition that says, 'If it's an animal eat it, if it's a woman make love to her and if it's a man sell him an Exocet.' The French say that frogs' legs taste a bit like chicken. They don't say which bit of the chicken. It's also why we call (used to call!) the French frogs. Just think if that unknown gourmet had decided to eat the leg of a bullock? That nickname would say it all.

★

F is also for **THE F-WORD,** Federal. Like the other more famous F-word, it's never uttered in mixed company, i.e., Brits and any other Europeans. This is a plan to create a Federal Europe with, it is feared, an elected President and a supreme governing body sitting in Brussels, or Berlin West, as it will then no doubt be called, telling us what to do. And taking no notice when we tell them what to do. Supporters of federation, who are trying to slip their plan in through the back door, are known as Federasts.

★

F is also for **A NUMBER OF OTHER EUROPEAN F-WORDS.** These words can give hours of simple pleasure on long motorway journeys to children of all ages. For instance, in Sweden drivers do a lot of farting (exiting from the motorway) and the Danes call their Parliament the Folketing, while the Dutch have Fokkink Bols.

G IS FOR GARIBALDI, the nineteenth-century Italian patriot who brought about the unification of Italy between shifts at the biscuit factory. Big G, who is one of Italy's greatest heroes (name two others) found immortality, and a place on the shelves of the world's supermarkets, the day he dropped a fly paper into the biscuit dough. Other famous Europeans who gave their names to foods include Bismarck (herring), Napoleon (cake) and Ivan the Terrible (airline food).

★

G is also for **GARLIC,** which is consumed in vast quantities by Continental Europeans. If you have ever wondered what it feels like to be an escargot in its shell, get in a hotel lift almost anywhere in Europe at eight o'clock in the morning with half a dozen fat and sweat-

ing Eurogluttons. It's a twenty Odor Eater job. Garlic is supposed to be very good for keeping away colds. It's not bad at keeping away people, either. And of course garlic has been used in Europe for centuries for warding off vampires. We don't have a history of vampires in Britain but we have all sorts of other bloodsuckers – Vatmen, tax inspectors, wheelclampers – maybe we should see if it works on them.

★

***G is also for* GENITALIA,** the private part of Alitalia.

***G is also for* GERMANY.**
Ten things you must never say to a German:

Thought your lads did well in the Gulf.

Do you know where I could get a decent salt beef sandwich?

I like Japanese cars.

I suppose you've got to sell your germ warfare factories to somebody.

Did you ever see that episode of *Fawlty Towers*? Hysterical.

That's my towel.

We have ways of making you talk.

Tell us a joke.

What's the German for 'dickhead'?

Pity about 1966.

***G is also for* GOEBBELS,** who was Hitler's PR man. If he was around today he'd be trying to get him a spot on *Wogan*. 'Tell Tel Adolf's got lots of funny stories. And he doesn't want to plug the book but he would like to show a couple of clips from *Heil de Heil,* his new camp sit com. One more thing. Tel's keen on golf, right? Nobody knows more about getting out of bunkers than my Adolf.'

***G is also for* GOLF** which is becoming increasingly popular. They are building so many golf courses in Europe now that it will soon be possible for British golfers to bore the arse off everybody in eleven other countries as well as this one. Some of the most spectacular courses are in Spain but keep a look-out for the natives unless you want to get a hole in Juan.

The rule at many European golf clubs is that you can buy a new ball for the equivalent of five pence but that lunch will cost you £45. They like to get you by

'Yes, I thought it was plankton too, but's its a load of bloody golf balls!'

the meals. There are some amazing clifftop courses in Portugal running alongside the Atlantic and at one of them the authors watched a German golfer unwrap a brand new Dunlop 65 ball at the first hole, tee it up and then slice it way out into the ocean. He took another brand new Dunlop 65, unwrapped it and sliced that into the Atlantic. He did this seven times, using a new ball every time. Finally his partner said to him, 'Why don't you put down an old ball?' He said, 'I've never had an old ball.'

G is also for GREECE.
Ten things you must never say to a Greek:

Got any Turkish coffee?

Have you lost your marbles?

Well, it started here, didn't it?

I think you should let them have Cyprus.

This houmous isn't as good as Marks and Sparks's.

What's the Greek for 'pederast'?

You don't mind if I call you 'Bubble'?

Were any of your family in the Colonel's torture squads?

If my dinner tasted like that I'd smash the plate as well.

The influence of Ancient Greece is everywhere, especially in the cooking. The Greeks love their lamb and they're also quite keen on it as food, and they stuff a lot of tomatoes, a habit that would get them arrested in most other countries. Greeks are a nation of seafarers, they were saying Hello sailor, or its Homeric equivalent, thousands of years before Portsmouth's finest.

In addition to the bulemic's friend, the post piss-up donor, the Greeks also gave the world geometry – Pythagoras was putting squares on triangles long before Paul gave Linda a job with Wings; comedy and the Archimedes Principle, which has now been superseded by the Oliver Reed Principle, which states that a body submerged in beer soon displaces its own volume out the back. The Greeks also gave the world the first bad joke – First Greek: Euripides? Second Greek: No, the dog did. First Greek: I don't wish to know that. Kindly leave the Parthenon. (*Bob's Big Book of Greek Philosopher Jokes*, Vol III).

Some people are at a loss to know what to say when they come across their first Greek ruin. A polite 'Not tonight thank you' should suffice. Vast tracts of Greece are covered with olive groves of which the Greeks are intensely proud. If they invite you round to spend an evening catching olives, don't ask Olive's what. The Greek Orthodox Church is famous for its ceremony with a great swinging and burning of incense. When you see one of the priests swinging an incense burner the correct procedure is to make the sign of the cross and not lean across and say 'Excuse me, sweetie, your handbag's on fire.'

As those of you who have been on Greek holidays, to distant Corfu, or, if you prefer, far Corfu, will know, the local tipple is retsina, which is often used in the making of cocktails, Molotov cocktails mostly, where they want something to beef up the petrol. Retsina,

which is also a very popular girl's name in Australia, has the side-effect of making men want to get up and dance with other men and generally behave like Zorba the Schmuck. Greek dancing is easily picked up, as are most people after a few glasses of retsina. Greek men tend to be on the small side – their statues confirm this – and buy lots of shoes with concealed raised heels, so beware of Greeks wearing lifts.

G is also for **GREEN,** which many Europeans are, indeed there is a Green political party in Germany with Green Members of Parliament. We have Greens in the House of Commons ... well we have a few stewed vegetables. The Eurogreens are trying to clean up the air of Eastern Europe where the factories belch out black smoke twenty-four hours a day. Their dream is to shut down the chimneys at night, thus stopping their nocturnal emissions, and confirming the view that many Eurogreens are teachers in Catholic boys' schools.

H IS FOR HAMBURG which is famous for the Reeperbahn, the Oxford Street of nookie, except that on the Reeperbahn the letters C and A probably don't mean coats and accessories. Germans, as a rule, and they do like to, are very upfront about sex. Quite a few of them are very outback as well. They have sex supermarkets with names like Knobs R Us, Sex U Like, Hairy Nichols and, for masochists, Marks and Spanker. They play songs like the Beach Boys' 'Good Vibrators' and they all have a fast checkout (five orgasms or less). But like all supermarkets, when you get to the checkout the girl on the till never knows the price of the one item in your basket you don't want anybody to know about. 'I'm sorry I don't know the price of that but I'll just find out. Helga, how much is the six-inch penis extension? No, white. *Danke*. Forty-five marks.'

Like the supermarkets in some of the trendier parts

of London, where romance has blossomed over the frozen peas, so sex supermarkets are a great place to meet the girl, or the man, of your naughty dreams. A girl filling her basket with condoms, for instance, is certainly worth chatting up. Ask her their yell-by date. On the other hand if you see a girl filling a basket with dozens of Extra-Life HP 11 batteries, don't waste your time. The shops have shelves of state-of-the-part sexual appliances – the ultimate in DIY sex.

Over there, B and Q means 'big and quick'. When the final trade barrier is removed presumably these sex supermarkets will open up in Britain (no more sending off to PO Boxes in Essex and hoping that the brown paper wrapper doesn't tear in the post again). They probably won't be located in the heart of shopping centres but on the fringes. They like to catch customers by the malls.

H is also for HAUSFRAU, which is German for house-wife, or house person. German housewives, or house persons, have a trade union and from time to time they go on strike, demanding special social security payments, pensions and third party insurance to cover them in case they ever catch their husbands with a third party.

H is also for HEAVEN. Heaven is where the weather is Mediterranean but the sea isn't, where German holi-

daymakers never get up until noon, where beer bellies, red sunburn and socks are a sexual turn-on, where the hotel gives you the same rate for your travellers cheques as the bank, where the Italians pinch their own bottoms, where the pigeons only bomb the French and where everybody speaks English.

★

***H is also for* HELL.** Hell is where the comedian's a Belgian, the chef's a Greek, the mini-cab driver's an Italian, the brain surgeon's Irish, the tailor's Bulgarian, the television controller's French, the pop singer's Norwegian, the Redcoat's German, the Car of the Year's a Skoda, the Page Three girl's an East German shot putter, the kiss of lifer's a Sicilian truck driver and *Neighbours* is on twenty-four hours a day, in Flemish.

★

***H is also for* HITLER,** who launched the German underarm deodorant industry in the thirties (slogan: 'See what a little squirt can do') and the forged diaries industry in the seventies and nineties. Hitler is still regarded as an OK guy in those parts of Germany where the shops, restaurants and hotels only take one credit card, MasterRace.

I IS FOR IMPOTENCE, which is expected to show an upturn, if you'll forgive the contradiction, after 1992 when hordes of power-dressed New Eurowomen (motto: Think German, Kiss French) will invoke the spirit of Joan of Arc and Attila the Nun and terrify the new Euromen (motto: I must get to Sainsbury's before they close) with their condom-crammed briefcases and demands for better money, better jobs, better this, that and the other. Actually, they won't be bothered about the other. The majority seem able to make their own arrangements, most of which appear to involve batteries of some sort.

The prospects of a tough male response to the march of the Eurosisterhood is not good. Addressing a private meeting of the Society of Cocky Randy Old Tossers and Undersized Men, SCROTUM, the Prince of Wales, in an unreported speech, compared the situation to the first time the distinguished American choreographer, Jerome Robbins, worked with a chorus of British male dancers on a production of *West Side Story*. After watching them flounce around the stage for some minutes, more Pets and Larks than Jets and Sharks, the dancing master stopped the rehearsal. 'Gentlemen,' he risked. 'I need more virility, more machismo; guys, I want to see some balls.' And a voice from the rear cried: 'Props!'

***I is also for* INSULTS** and if, as a New European, you feel you've been ripped off, set up, stitched up or carved up, then you can take your case to the European Court of Justice at The Hague. Be specific with your lawyer about the court you want. Don't be vague, ask for ...

***I is also for* INSULTS** (see JOKES).

★

***I is also for* INTEREST RATES,** the knickers of the economy: people are only happy when they're coming down. Once upon a time, in those dim and distant days when the pound was still worth 25p, it seemed to us that interest rates were something the Bank of England dreamed up to mess us about. Now the Eurobankers, a right load of bankers, are throwing in their ten pfennigs' worth. But whatever happens to our interest rates, you can be sure that we'll go on paying the banks a lot more than they'll ever pay us. That's why in a

war, tank corps commanders like to have their leading
tanks manned by men from NatWest, Barclays and the
Midlands – nobody charges the way they do.

***I is also for* INTERPOL,** which is not Interflora's sister
organization ('Say it with parrots'), but the organization which hunts down criminals who cross national
borders. And talking of crossing, what do you get if you
cross a Swiss with an Italian? Somebody who makes
cuckoo clocks with hair under the wings. What do
you get if you cross a German with a Frenchman?
Somebody who gets up at dawn and leaves a woman on
your sunbed. What do you get if you cross a Belgian
with a Dane? Not a lot.

***I is also for* IRELAND.**
Ten things you should never say to an Irishman:

Does the priest know you're doing this?

Does your mother know you're doing this?

You should try English Guinness.

Didn't I see you in Piccadilly last week – digging it
up?

Step outside and say that.

Can you tell me how to get to...?

Ever thought of wearing black shoes with a blue
suit?

I never tell Irish jokes. There were these two China-
men, Paddy and Mick....

You'd really like to be English, wouldn't you?

Can I buy you a drink?

★

***I is also for* ITALY.**
Ten things you must never say to an Italian:

Got any Heinz spaghetti?

Is that true about Italian tanks?

Who's Prime Minister today?

Call yourself a driver?

I fancy your sister.

He dived.

What part of France does Chianti come from?

Do you know that George Formby wrote a song about
Mussolini? 'Hanging from a Lamp-post by the
Corner of the Street.'

What's the Italian for 'don't point that thing at me'?

You sure you're not gay?

What you say about Italians depends on where you are
in the world. In Britain, for instance, when we think
of Italians we think of ice-cream, footballers who could
get a job at the National Theatre, waiters in red shirts

and tight trousers (as the Queen Mother once said, 'What an interesting place to keep the olives'), opera singers, great heaps of pasta, and opera singers who look like great heaps of pasta. Pasta is believed to have been brought back to Italy from China by Marco Polo, who thereby not only gave the world spag bol but also the Chinese takeaway. (Though you won't find it in many history books, Marco Polo had a Scandinavian cousin, Bjorn Polo, who invented open-cast mining. He

was known as the Swede With The Hole.) But in the United States you don't tell jokes about Italians unless you have an overwhelming compulsion to end up reinforcing a block of concrete on the bottom of the Hudson River. The same goes for Sicily where walls have ears. Some of them have noses and chins as well, where the bodies didn't fall far enough into the cement. The most famous Godfather of them all was THE Godfather, Don Corleone, who got fatter and fatter on huge meals of liver and kidneys cooked by his daughter. She kept making an offal he couldn't refuse.

The current reigning Godfathers, current, that is, at the time of writing, are a warm sounding bunch. They are Carmine 'The Furious' Alfieri, Burt Bacharach's inspiration for 'What's It All About, Alfieri', Salvatore 'Shorty' Riini, Michele 'Crazyman' Zaza, Michele 'The Pope' Greco, God's hit man on Earth, and Gennaro 'Swanny' Licciardi. Good names for dropping if you ever get caught speeding in Sicily. You can invent your own Mafiosi, all it requires is a menu from an Italian restaurant. It's amazing the 'the made men' you'll find among the dishes. For instance Vitello Con Fungi is obviously a hit man, so are Focaccia di Manuelinia and Spigola al Limone while Lumaconi con Nocci e Mascarpone is obviously the Godfather's consigliere.

J IS FOR JAPAN, which is not a member of the
Common Market but is busy building so many factories
in Britain that she might as well be. It's thought a lot
of Japanese money has gone into the Channel Tunnel,
though they would have preferred some other means.
They kept saying to the British: 'Build a bridge, build
a bridge.' The great fear amongst most Europeans is
not that the Japanese will flood Europe with cars, TV
sets and pocket stereos (the Sony Bonkman for Italy,
the Sony Marchman for Germany and the Sony Onion-
man for France), but that they will buy up the place
and turn it into a golf course. Why not? It's what
they're doing everywhere else. But even as we write,
or as you read, a committee in Brussels is considering
what to do about Japan's role in the New Europe and,
not unnaturally, Japan would like to sit on the com-

COMMITTEE
ROOM

'It's all very well these chaps wanting to be on the committee!'

mittee. Actually they'd like to send over a sumo wres-
tler to sit on it. Or rather, all over it.

J is also for **JOGGING.** Running has always been something they've done a lot of in Europe, though some countries have done more than others. German women jog a lot but then most German women have a lot to jog. What do you call a jogger in the Swiss Alps? Barmy.

***J is also for* JOKES.** Every nationality in the world has a nationality it jokes about. The British tell jokes about the Irish, the Irish tell jokes about the Kerries, the Americans tell jokes about the Canadians. 'What's the worst-selling book in the United States? *Canada, Our Dear Neighbour To The North.* The Americans tell jokes about the Poles. How can you tell the bride at a Polish wedding? She's the one with the plaited armpits. And not only the Poles. An Irishman, a Pole and a Puerto Rican jumped from the top of the Empire State Building. Who hit the ground first? The Irishman, he went straight down. The Pole lost his way and the Puerto Rican had to stop and spray 'Screw you motherf——' on the side of the building.

The Canadians tell Newfies – jokes about New-foundlanders. How do you get a Newfie to burn his ear? Phone him while he's ironing his trousers. How do you get him to burn the other one? Call him back.

The Italians tell jokes about the Albanians. A wealthy Italian businessman bought the latest electronic toy from Japan, an alarm clock that worked on IQ. Before you went to sleep you simply set it to the IQ you wanted to be wakened by. The first night he set it to 120 and the next morning he was wakened by a voice saying: 'Good morning. It's a lovely day but take an umbrella, I think it's going to rain later.' He thought what a wonderful machine. The next night he set the IQ at 140 and the next morning he was wakened by the same voice saying: 'Good morning it's a lovely day again. You have a dental appointment at eleven a.m.; I've telephoned your secretary to remind you.' Amazing. That night he set the IQ at 180, genius rating. The next morning the voice wakened him with: 'The market's gone crazy in Japan, sell every share you have and put the money into pesetas.' He couldn't believe it. The next night out of curiosity he set the IQ at 80. The following morning he was wakened by an Albanian.

The French tell jokes about the Belgians, and the Belgians tell jokes about the Walloons. It must be bad enough being a Walloon without having a Belgian telling jokes about you. But in the new, all-singing, all-dancing Europe will these jokes be banned by the new Eurojoke Commission (courtesy of The People's Republics of Islington and Camden)? Will squads of Eurojoke police in unmarked Skodas with sirens that go 'Ha Ha. Ha Ha' surround our minds and shout through loudhailers, 'O.K., joke we know you're in there. Throw out your pun and come out with your punchline in the air.'?

After 1992 will a sauerkraut be just a kind of cabbage and not a miserable old sod from Düsseldorf? Will there be no more Italian jokes? Why does an Italian tank have four reverse gears and one forward? In case they attack from behind. What do you say to an Italian in a suit and tie? A table for two, please. Who gives the bride away at an Italian wedding? Nobody. They all keep their mouths shut. Italians make wonderful waiters. If I send them the wool could they make me one? The Italians are fiercely proud of their virility and always do well in the Eurovision Dong Contest. Last year's winners, Luigi and Gennaro went on to the world finals in Sydney, Australia. They're very big down under. They were crossing the Sydney Harbour Bridge on the way to the stadium where the finals were being held, when Luigi said: 'I've got to take a leak,' and Gennaro said, 'Good idea, I'll have one as well.' And so they stood, having a leak, on the Sydney

Harbour Bridge. After about thirty seconds Gennaro said, 'Hey that water's really cold' and Luigi said, 'And deep.'

But even if Brussels does bring in laws banning the telling of jokes about a fellow member, as opposed to a fellow's member, which is something they'll never pull off, we think the jokes will still go on.

K IS FOR KNOCKE LE ZOOT, which is what Belgians do every time they see Jonathan Ross on television. (Jonathan is very popular in Belgium where they think he's a bit of Walloon. Or a wally.) People on the other side of the Channel watch a lot of British television, and they all have the same favourite comedy show, *Prime Minister's Question Time*. Most of them think *'Allo, 'Allo* is a documentary, and the burghers of Delft, a sad crowd who are known as the miserable burghers of Delft, want to erect a monument to Jeremy Beadle in the town square. When it's built they're going to invite him over, and drop it on him.

★

K is also for **KRAUT,** one of the those words we won't be using any more. If you're not familiar with it, kraut

is a term of endearment, a word we used to use to convey that special warmth and affection we feel for our German brothers, e.g., two's company, three's a kraut.

L IS FOR LAGER, which Europeans drink by the bucket and Brits throw up in the bucket. There are probably a hundred different brands of lager in Europe but they all retain some characteristic of the country where they were brewed, which usually emerges when people drink too much of them. For instance, if you get bombed on German lager you dream of world domination. If you get looped on Belgian lager you dream of winning the Tour de France. If you get smashed on French lager you dream of making love all night. If you get rat-arsed on British lager you don't have time to dream. You're too busy waking up and going to the loo. Britain has lager louts, Germany has lager lauts, Greece has retsina rowdies (they have terrible hang-unders), Italy has Chianti crazies and France has the Macon Mob, a bunch of guys who go out and get smashed on cheap red and end up pissed as Nuits.

'Can I borrow your bucket, mate?'

★

L is also for **LAWYERS.** The one group who can be sure of plenty of employment in the New Europe. More rules, more regulations, more laws are going to mean more lawyers. In this, at least, the United States of Europe (arrggh: Mrs Thatcher makes the Sign of the Cross with her forefingers and holds it up in front of her; Nicholas Ridley takes up smoking again) will be emulating the United States of America where everybody either is a lawyer, is training to become a lawyer, is sleeping with a lawyer or is calling a lawyer. America has lawyers the way · we have social workers. In America Peggy Sue isn't just a song title, it's an instruction.

The jokes they're telling in America, they'll soon be telling in Europe. What do you call twenty lawyers floating face-down in the Rhine? A start. Why did Brussels get all the lawyers and Naples get all the dung beetles? Naples had first choice. What do you get if you cross a lawyer with a taxidermist? A guy who stuffs everybody. What do you get if you cross a German lawyer with a British barrister? Herr in the briefs. How do you know you've been mugged by a Swiss lawyer? No marks.

We presume that after 1992 the member countries will retain their own criminal code. In France this will be the Napoleonic Code, whereas in Britain we shall stick with the Inspector Morse Code. But presumably it will only be a matter of time before there will be one Central Criminal Court in some place like Strasbourg, and the Old Bailey will be closed down and reopened as a shopping centre, which is how most villains see it anyway. In this new Central Eurocourt countries will be allotted their own courtroom (Norvège Un Court) and Britain will insist that all the trials are conducted in English, which is only fair as we'll probably be involved in most of them.

★

L is also for **LEGENDS.** Europe has more old legends than a Japanese car dealer in July. For instance, Thor, the god of burst pipes; Wotan, the god of bronzed females, and Lorelei a fabulous female siren who sat upon a rock in the Rhine and lured sailors to their doom. She's still doing it today. From a bar stool in Hamburg. There was Joan of Arc who perished in the flames, though being in France her stake was under-done. And there was Luther who lived on a Diet of Worms, which is why he was probably always constipated. In Denmark they revere Gorm The Old who sounds like a character from *Monty Python* but was, in fact, Denmark's first king. He had a son called Harold Bluetooth, believed to be the original Danish Blue, who in turn had a son called Sweyn Forkbeard. This policy of being named after one's outstanding physical feature was abandoned upon the birth of Kristian the Huge. Little is known about the royal daughters, Helga Greatarse and Ingeborge D-Cup. There are lesser known legends you may encounter, Pilsner the Incontinent, the first wet; Mungo the Remarkable, the patron saint of pawnbrokers, and Hainault The Flatulent, the Visigoth general who always led from the rear, at his troops' request.

★

L is also for LIGHTBULB.

Here are some European lightbulb jokes:

How many Belgian alcoholics does it take to change a lightbulb? All of them, but the lightbulb's got to get smashed as well.

How many German hookers does it take to change a lightbulb? One. But the lightbulb's got to wear a condom.

How many Italians does it take to change a lightbulb? None, they're too busy changing governments to change lightbulbs.

How many Eurocrats does it take to change a lightbulb? Before we answer that, does this lightbulb conform to EC Regulation X4J112K or is it shrimp-flavoured?

How many Spaniards does it take to change a lightbulb? Two: one to hold the bulb, the other to finish wiring the building.

How many Albanians does it take to change a lightbulb? What's a lightbulb?

How many Greeks does it take to change a lightbulb? Twenty – and the lightbulb's got to be dim as well.

How many Common Market Commissioners does it take to change a lightbulb? It doesn't matter how many, they'll still screw it up.

L is also for LUFTHANSA AND LUFTWAFFE, Germany's airline and airforce. This week, Hans Gruner, Luf-

thansa's last remaining World War II Luftwaffe pilot, retired. You always knew when Hans was at the controls. Whenever he got close to London he would put the plane in a steep dive, open the luggage compartment, bomb St Paul's with Samsonite and then turn round and fly back to Berlin. His most spectacular achievement took place over the Atlantic. The passengers on a 747 to New York had just finished watching the movie when they heard Hans's voice on the tannoy. 'If those of you sitting on the right-hand side of the aircraft would care to look out of their windows they will see that the far engine is on fire. There is absolutely nothing to worry about. We have three other engines.' Ten minutes later, Hans spoke again. 'If passengers on the left-hand side of the aircraft would care to look out of their windows they will see that the other far engine is now on fire. There is absolutely nothing to worry about. This plane can fly perfectly safely on two engines.' Ten minutes later Hans was back again. 'If all passengers look out of the windows you will now see that both the remaining engines are on fire. And if you look down to the ocean, 39,000 feet below, you will see a tiny yellow speck. That speck is a rubber dinghy. I am speaking to you from that dinghy.' One of the best known Luftwaffe planes in World War II was the Fokker, a very popular plane with pilots and comedians. There are still lots of Fokkers flying today, including all those lucky Fokkers who get cheap tickets in Irish bucket shops.

L is also for **LUXEMBOURG,** the famous radio station

which is also a country. A very small country that makes a lot of noise. It's the Bonnie Langford of Europe.

Here are ten things you must never say to a native of Luxembourg:

Doesn't apply. You can say anything you like to a native of Luxembourg.

M IS FOR MARADONA, whose 'Hand of God' put England out of the World Cup and whose nose of coke put him out of football altogether. Maradona's fondness for the Devil's Dandruff, for Lucifer's Snuff, for the Latin American Dancing Powder, became apparent when he was playing for Naples and instead of kicking off he'd drop to his knees and start trying to snort up the centre line.

Maradona has announced that he's going to devote the rest of his life to teaching young footballers everything he knows, plus a couple of things he ought to learn himself, like: always get somebody else to carry your stash through customs. Maradona was probably fingered by an abandoned pusher; they hate it when somebody goes off and sticks their nose into someone else's business.

★

M is also for **MEDITERRANEAN,** which somebody once described as like swimming in a warm bath – and when something particularly disgusting floats past your nose you do feel as though you're back in the bathroom. Some people think it's a disgrace that countries pour raw sewage into the Med. Others are relieved it hasn't been put on their plates first. Experts advise us to be careful about eating fish from the Mediterranean, avoid brown mullet, for instance, or muckerel or unexploded shellfish. It's a bit unfair to say that we shouldn't trust fish from the Med, surely they're the ones who shouldn't be trusting us – must be like living your whole life in an underwater Trafalgar Square.

But what, we hear you cry, can be done to clean up the Med? The answer is simple. We, the British, should go to Brussels and tell all the Eurocrats, the MEPs and the Commissioners how much we like the Mediterranean as it is and how we would treat any efforts to change it as a direct attack on our sovereignty and sufficient reason for us to re-consider whether we want to remain in Europe. The Med would be sparkling within a month.

M is also for **MERDE.** This is a favourite French expletive. In French streets people use it all the time unlike British streets where people tread in it all the time.

M is also for **MISTRESS,** once described as the bit

between the Mrs and the mattress. In this context it has nothing to do with school mistress, though strict discipline may be a part of her duties. For our younger readers who find it hard to grasp the concept of the mistress, it's an old-fashioned idea, much loved in France where businessmen and politicians are almost expected to keep a mistress to do all those things they could never dream of asking the mother of their children to do. Like iron a shirt.

A projected move by the EC to introduce regulations for mistresses, e.g., regarding bust, hip and waist measurements, proximity of upper leg to armpit, time off, as opposed to time spent having it off, security of position or positions, clothes allowance (nurses' uniforms, gym slips, SS outfits), proper training in the cleaning of ceiling mirrors and in the operation of any special equipment (pulleys, nooses, Black and Decker industrial polishers), was abandoned after two million Albanians turned up in Brussels seeking jobs as inspectors. The idea of the mistress as one of the trappings of a successful middle age has never really caught on in Britain where sex is still regarded as something to be punished rather than celebrated, as Lord Lambton and Sir Ralph Halpern know. (What do you get if you cross a canned fruit tycoon with Sir Ralph Halpern? A man from Del Monte who says yes five times a night.)

★

M is also for **MONTE CARLO,** where some of the richest people in the world hang out. Unfortunately the richest people in the world are not the most attractive people in the world and what they hang out is disgusting. The harbour at Monte Carlo is where the owners of some of the world's most fabulous private yachts like to tie up. And sometimes be tied up themselves. When a girl is praised in Monte Carlo for her long lashes, they're not talking eye make-up. Nowhere else in the world will you see so many beautiful, smooth, tanned, firm young bodies servicing so many wrinkled old scrotums.

Wrinkled old rich scrotums that is. The sort of characters who spell bisexual 'buy'. If that kind of social work appeals to you (it's not so much Help the Aged, more Help the Aged Do It), then there are plenty of openings in Monte Carlo.

Monte Carlo also has its share of rich old ladies who know how to hang on to their youth. They give him a new Rolex every twenty minutes, make sure they keep him laughing all the way to the bonk. They describe these male bimbos as secretaries; what they take down certainly isn't shorthand. One rich old lady was asked if there was a going rate for the job. She said, 'No, it's more a coming and going rate.' The young men – like most studs, they spend a lot of time rolling under the bed – are philosophical about their role, and their roll. One quoted a celebrated American gynaecologist who, when asked what he did, said, 'I'm just a spreader of old wives' tails.'

N IS FOR NAPOLEON, the French Emperor who was named after a bottle of brandy, unlike many Frenchmen who were conceived after a bottle of brandy. For all his military campaigns Napoleon was terrible at geography – he didn't know his Alsace from his Elba. In the imperial sack, according to the Empress Josephine, Napoleon was no great shakes, but then neither are most Arab princes. 'Not tonight, Josephine' he would say, as he unstrapped his corset and put his teeth in a glass by the side of the bed. 'I've got to be at Waterloo first thing in the morning.' An excuse still used by commuters today.

Nobody knows much about Napoleon's personal hygiene (a dirty Nappy?) but traditionally Frenchmen hardly ever washed, cleaned their teeth or used deodorants. In the words of the American radio commercials of the forties, 'It may be December outside but it's

'You've gone off me, chérie, I can tell.'

always August beneath your armpits'. No charmpits, those armpits. Somebody once said that a bar of soap to a Frenchman was like a cross to Dracula. (Joke: How do you get a Frenchman out of the bath? Put soap and water in it.) The image of the romantic Frenchman is, 'ow they say in France, crappe. A report published this year said that three months after the wedding

French husbands stopped shaving at the weekends, never changed their underwear or their socks, did nothing but overeat and drink and expected everything to be done for them. Maybe we've got more in common than we thought.

N is also for NETHERLANDS.
Ten things you must never say to a Dutchman:

Want to hear a joke about a dyke?

If it hadn't been for Max Bygraves who would have heard of you?

My wife's got one of your caps.

Yeah, but who taught you how to play football?

Freed any IRA men recently?

Wait till we have some Molluccans on trial in Britain.

And who's the real star, your wife or the donkey?

If there's one thing, I hate more than tulips it's Edam.

What's the Dutch for 'sanctimonious old fart'?

The country's dull because it's flat, but what's your excuse?

N is also for NEW EUROPEAN which is what we are all going to become. The New European will show Dutch courage, take French leave, wear Italian clothes and

drive a German car, available in only two colours, Danish blue or Belgian chocolate. He'll build castles in Spain which he'll sell as time-shares, have the luck of the Irish, never Welsh on his friends and every night he'll lie back and think of England. But all these parts go to make a whole, which is precisely what many people think we're in danger of disappearing into.

O IS FOR OBSTRUCTIVE AND OFFICIAL, two words that were made for each other. There are going to be thousands of obstructive officials in the New Europe telling us what to put in our sausages, what to call our beer, what elastic to put in our knickers. Lately they have been having a go at office pin-ups. No more big boobies on factory walls, say the big boobies in Brussels. They don't know what they're doing. It's only because of the Page Three girl on the calendar that half the workforce of Britain know what month it is.

★

O is also for **OFFAL,** a Scottish word as in 'Jings, this tastes offal.' On the Continent they eat an offal lot of offal and can't understand why we don't eat it as well. It invariably tastes delicious so our advice would be:

eat it and don't worry about what's in it. In other words treat it like fast food hamburger.

O is also for OMELETTE, which is Danish for Shakespeare's best-known play. They say you can't make an omelette without breaking eggs. We know a couple of motorway service stations where they're having a bloody good try.

★

O is also for **ONAN,** a small village in the Pyrenees where the adult male population have all gone blind.

★

O is also for **OPERA,** which, as everybody knows, is never over until the fat lady sings. Opera is supposed to be for the élite but that's just a rumour put round by people who can't afford the tickets. People think nothing of paying a hundred pounds, and up, for a ticket to the opera. (We don't think much of it either). One woman paid £105 to see a performance of *La Bohème* and when she heard that Mimi's tiny hand was frozen she said, 'At the prices we're paying they could afford to buy her gloves.'

Opera is very popular in Europe where it's sometimes put on as an alternative to entertainment. One of the biggest names in opera is Luciano Pavarotti, a man who fills the world's biggest stadia. On his own. Pavarotti is a national hero in Italy. They want to name a mountain after him, but they can't find one big enough. His singing of 'Nessun Dorma' for the 1990 World Cup was sensational, if confusing. The aria comes from an opera called *Turandot* and after it was sung in a recent production at Covent Garden a small boy in the audience called out, 'Oh good, now the football's going to start.' The Italians love opera almost as much as they love football. Actually, the two are very similar. Opera has divas, football has divers.

Turandot was written by Puccini, who, along with his fellow countrymen, Verdi and Rossini, composed some of the world's most beautiful music which is finally getting the sort of public recognition it deserves and being paid the highest tribute the twentieth century can bestow. It's being used for backing tracks on TV commercials. Rossini, who wrote the theme tune for *The Lone Ranger,* also wrote *The Barber of Seville,* which contains one of the most moving moments in all opera when the barber sings 'Nessun dorma con un pachetto di gianni', which, roughly translated, means, 'And was there something for the weekend, sir?' But be warned that opera in Europe is not for the faint-hearted. It's violent and loud. Hearts are broken, women are carelessly tossed to one side, lovers are left abandoned. And that's just trying to get a drink at the interval.

★

O is also for **ORGASM.** At the time of writing, the European Commissioners have no plans to introduce a standardized Eurorgasm. There's nothing in the pipe-line, so to speak. However, rather like the orgasm itself, it's only a matter of time. Consider the prospect, some committee of Eurocrats will determine how many are permissible and with what frequency; they will issue broad guidelines (especially useful in Norfolk), defining acceptable degrees of intensity, and they will also list a number of mental exercises which may be used by the male to slow down the process, e.g., repeating the Common Market regulations governing the milk yield of dairy cattle with regard to specific rebates and surpluses related to, but not excluding, farm support payments under existing EC mechanisms. They will also supply a list of fantasy figures, i.e. if you have to think of somebody else, Brussels will tell you who it can be. Faking it will be banned. Especially by men.

Brussels will also probably introduce a tax on orgasms, a sort of pay as you yearn. When the members

'There's that dreadful man in the next valley yodelling again — is he never *satisfied!'*

of the EuroBonking Committee have finished they'll light a cigarette, lie back and ask each other 'How was it for you?'

As far as the Big 0 goes, there doesn't appear to be any significant difference between the member countries, though some nations are noisier than others. In Switzerland, for instance, the exultant cries can often be heard in the next valley. This is how yodelling started. The Italians are like their cars, they make a lot of noise and like to burn rubber. The famous aria from Verdi's *Aida* is believed to have been inspired by the couple in the flat downstairs. They're quieter in Northern Europe. Even when they're being laid back Scandinavian girls are laid back. A woman in France claims to have clocked up 134 orgasms in an hour, which is more than two a minute, and, if true, could lead to a lot of terrified men in bedrooms throughout Britain and the rest of Europe. I expect she'll end up in the *Guinness Book of Records,* alongside the baked bean eaters and the egg throwers. We can't wait to see David Frost try to break that record on TV.

P IS FOR PARIS, a city that's great to get plastered in. Bob Hope used to say that Paris was the city where they had signs in all the shop windows saying 'French spoken here'. However, don't bother trying. The Parisians delight, whether they are waiters, hotel switchboard operators or shop assistants, in letting you ask for something in perfect French that you've spent hours learning from a tape, and then answering you in English. Bastards. If, for some reason, you're caught shoplifting in Paris, it could be the menopause or PMT, though judges are loath to accept these excuses from men, the best thing to do is jump in the river and plead 'Guilty but in-Seine'. (That joke came off the back of a match box in 1923, and it was old then.)

Parisian women are fantastically elegant but very, very thin. Lots of chic but not much cheek. Not too comfortable in bed but wonderful for making soup. Gay

Paree still is, in places, though the *Folies Bergère,* which once seemed so naughty, is now so tame you could take your granny to see it, in fact these days you might see your granny in it. The Folies are like English girls. They look terrific with their clothes off and they never move. Something their husbands have known for years.

But there are still some exotic houses of pleasure. One Englishman was fond of frequenting a famous such establishment on the Left Bank. One night as he was leaving Madame gave him five thousand francs. He said, 'What's this for?' She explained, 'I have a number of old clients who are no longer active and while you were taking your pleasure tonight I permitted a dozen of them to watch through a two-way mirror. I hope you are not offended.' Not at all, said the Englishman and went off into the night with his money. As he was leaving the next time Madame handed him twenty thousand francs. 'Twenty thousand?' he asked. She explained, 'After the last time so many people wanted to come that tonight I let fifty watch through the two-way mirror.' Again the Englishman went off into the night. As he was leaving the next time Madame handed him one million francs. 'Why so much?' he said. Madame beamed, 'a télévision français.'

★

P is also for **PASTA,** which comes in various shapes and sizes, as do the Italians who consume vast quantities of it. Some years ago *Panorama* tried to fool the nation with a report about the spaghetti harvest. Of course it was a hoax, an April Fool's joke. In Ireland, however, a farmer took it seriously and planted four hundred

WHAT ARE YOU GOING TO FERTILIZE WITH, GAFFER, TOMATO SAUCE?

tins of spaghetti. Only two of them came up. Pasta is frequently on the menu at Number 10. They serve it with a normally reliable Whitehall sauce.

P is also for PEPAIUOLA, which is Italian for peppermill and penis substitute. Italian waiters all have long peppermills which they whip out and wave in front of their female customers, as if to say, 'What do you think of this then? How'd you like to come home to one of these every night?' Some women think it's not to be sneezed at. Wiser ones know that encouraging a peppermill flasher can only end in a terrible grind.

***P is also for* PERRIER**, the world's best-known mineral water, all of whose salesmen have at least three 'eau' levels. When Perrier had to withdraw their product from the world's supermarkets after it was found to be contaminated, the company chairman asked their advertising agency to help. The agency came up with a picture of an empty Perrier bottle with words 'eau f——'. Perrier didn't buy it.

There are hundreds of different mineral waters in Europe, some of them passed by the local authority while others just come straight out of the ground. Doubtless Brussels will soon tell us what mineral waters we may or may not drink (Dean Martin would never touch water. He said fish f—— in it), but in the meantime, shop around because some of them have quite a kick. France, with its many atomic power stations is now selling nuclear mineral water (Eau Shit!). A friend of ours brought some back and served it at dinner one night with a main course of pork and beans. He got a phone call at midnight from one of his guests wanting to know what was in the mineral water. 'Where are you?' said our friend. The guest said, 'I'm in a phone box just across the road from where Harrods used to be.'

***P is also for* PIRATES** who roam Europe offering cheap versions of luxury goods like Cartier watches, Gucci shoes and Lacoste polo shirts. (This only applies to Western Europe. In Eastern Europe luxury goods are potatoes.) These pirates insist they are selling the genuine article but the discerning shopper will spot certain flaws. On a genuine Lacoste shirt the alligator is not standing on its head, Cartier is not spelt with a 'K' and there's no 'h' in Gucci.

These villains also do a nice line in pirate videos, changing their labelling from country to country. In Greece, for instance, *The Silence of the Lambs* is described as the story of a lucky shepherd. And they pirate CDs. Again, read the labels. A friend was going through a pile of classical CDs on a market stall in Athens when he came across 'Piano Concerto No 1 by Tchaikofsky'. He said to the guy running the stall, 'There's no 'f' in Tchaikovsky.' And the guy said, 'There'sa no sodding Beethoven either.'

***P is also for* PISA.** If you want to see the Leaning Tower while it's still leaning you'd better hurry because the tower is righting itself. Experts think it could be straight by the year 2000. It'll be one of the few things that is. The authorities point out that the tower is hundreds of years old. No wonder it's losing the inclination.

***P is also for* PISSOIR,** the name given to those quaint French street lavatories, in over-wrought iron, where you could see the heads and shoulders and the feet of *les artistes du pissoir,* as some of them undoubtedly were. Sadly the pissoir is being replaced by the Euro-supaloos which really are the business when it comes to doing the business. About the only thing they don't do is press your suit while you're waiting. However, coming soon is the Kawasaki Krapper, the new Japanese Suparoo, employing state of the (f)art lavatory technology. No more loo rolls, no more flushing. This beauty beats as it sweeps as it cleans.

★

P is also for **PISTE,** which thousands of Brits now go on every year. And some of them go skiing as well. (*More On The Piste Jokes,* Vol II, 1987). From being a pastime for the rich and leisured (fifteen years or so ago they were the only people, apart from plumbers, who went away in the winter), it's now a sport for the people. Well, most of the people. For while the Henrys and Carolines have now been joined on the slopes by the Simons and Emmas, the Sharons and Traceys haven't got there yet ('I'd love to go skiing, Trace, I really would. But it's all snow, init? Be nowhere to put me 'andbag down and I'd never be able to go to the loo with them things on me feet.').

More and more people are staying in chalets where 'gels from good families' – the sort who think cake is something one drinks, unless they're naughty gels when it's something one stuffs up one's hooter – spend their winters making beds, serving tea and cooking dinners for a succession of double-glazing salesmen, kitchen fitters, local government officers and their girlfriends from Wolverhampton and Milton Keynes, who spend their days falling down in the snow and their nights falling down in the street. They drink gallons of glühwein, the world's only curried wine. It's hot and you've no idea what they put in it. Their hero is Eddie the Eagle and they make lots of on-the-piste jokes.

But there is one thing a male skiBrit fears above all others, even above dropping his duty frees on the ice outside Munich Airport or finding a tree appearing between his legs at forty mph, and that's a handsome ski instructor. The one who looks like Robert Redford and wiggles his bum like Julian Clary. And who's driving all the women in his ski-class crazy, including the one he came with. There's not a lot to be done. Whether they're Swiss, Austrian, French or Italian, ski instructors always look the way that you know you're never going to look, no matter how many lessons you take. Like good Irish convent girls, their legs are always together. Bastards. All you can do is console yourself with the thought that if you put one in a suit from the Next Catalogue and dropped him, very heavily, in your local wine bar on a Friday none of the women would give him a second look. A fella might. On the other hand, you could just kick him in the Rossignols and stuff his ski poles up his Brenner.

Painful though it is to admit it, there are some things the Europeans do better than the British. Skiing is one of them. Frenchmen like to ski with their skis apart, they don't want to damage the equipment. The Germans like to bomb down the slopes. Old habits die hard.

Wherever you go in the Alps you'll see five-year-olds racing down the slopes, and you think they must have been born wearing skis. And then you see the pained

look on their mothers' faces and realize they probably were.

Some enthusiasts believe that skiing is more fun than sex: you can do it all day, nobody laughs if you're a beginner and when you get to the bottom you just turn round and have another go. Next winter, the BBC are launching a new ski programme to be hosted by Britain's best-known skier, Fergie. They're going to call it Ski Sunday. And Monday. And Tuesday. And . . .

***P is also for* POLICE,** also known, amongst other things, as polizei, carabinieri, gendarmerie or le nique-nique, who are soon to be immortalized in a new BBC series *'Allo, 'Allo, 'Allo.* If you get done for speeding in Germany you could try telling the rotten bastard, or Bulle, as they call him, that you are a 'dicker Fisch'. This doesn't mean you're hung like a mackerel but that you are a big shot. Unlike the jovial British bobby with his cheerful smile and love of practical jokes (see West Midlands Serious Crime Squad) your average Eurocop is not a big chuckler and won't appreciate being asked the German/Italian/Belgian for 'fascist pig'. Nor is he likely to believe you if you tell him that two fingers held in the air is a sign of admiration often used by the Brits towards their own police especially on festive occasions like poll tax riots.

***P is also for* PORTUGAL.**
Ten things you must never say to a Portuguese:

I thought you were Spanish.

Benfica are crap.

Have you tried rich ruby VP port?

They say you lot make wonderful servants.

Were you in the secret police?

Have you tried Valderma?

Bet you wish you could afford a holiday in the Algarve.

What's the Portuguese for 'pushy little bugger'?

'Then there's this one, that's a sign of admiration too.'

Are all the women in Lisbon Lisbians?

Name five famous Portuguese.

Portugal, we're often being reminded by some politician with a fondness for port and a free trip to Lisbon in his back pocket (strictly business of course, as a member of a Parliamentary delegation invited by an Anglo-Portuguese friendship society to study late night eating habits in Lisbon), is England's oldest ally and the two countries have enjoyed a 'special relationship' for more than six hundred years. Try using this when you find yourself negotiating an evening's entertainment. 'Special price for the special relationship?' That's when you'll probably learn the Portuguese for 'get stuffed'.

Q IS FOR QUEEN. There are a lot of queens in Europe, especially in Amsterdam at the weekends. The tallest royal queen is Margrethe of Denmark who is six feet tall in the royal socks and is known as The Great Dane. The quietest is Fabiola, who sounds like some Wet 'n' Stick plastic wallcovering but is, in fact, the Queen of the Belgians. Euroqueens like to be thought of as just one of the crowd and when a foreign Head of State unexpectedly drops in for tea, they think nothing of hopping on their bike and popping down to the local supermarket for a small brown, a packet of cheese spread and some of Mr Kipling's chocolate fancies. To our certain knowledge, our Queen has never hopped on a bike (she might have been carefully lowered on to one at Sandringham) and certainly not to nip down to Mr Patel's Buy-Rite at Victoria to stock up on the groceries. The Queen does not behave like one of the common herd. She leaves that to the younger royals.

At the time of writing there is a campaign to get the Queen to pay income tax. In anticipation of this we understand she's investigating three courses of action: putting the country in her husband's name; registering it as an oil tanker in Panama or employing Ken Dodd

as her tax consultant. If the Queen has to pay PAYR (Pay As You Reign) her deductions will make fascinating reading: Dog food £10m; Hay for horses, £20m; cartridges for shotguns, £10m; cigarettes for intruders, £5m; hire of husband's uniforms and medals (for flypasts, etc.), £2m; supply of tabloid press cuttings (Fergie, Princess Michael, Prince Edward etc.), £10m. Another Royal with vast holdings is the Queen of the Netherlands but apparently she's going on a diet.

But what will become of the Queen when Europe is finally united? Easy. She should be made Empress of

Europe. We don't suppose she would object. True, there would be another dozen or so openings of Parliament to attend, but she could use the same speech for each of them, nobody would notice the difference, and she'd enjoy the trooping of the colours of Benetton, especially as there'll be no colours worth trooping here. Critics of the scheme point out that other crowned heads might want to claim the European throne. No problem. They can do what they've done for centuries, fight over it.

Q is also for **QUOTAS**, which are a big turn-on for Eurocrats. They're always massaging their statistics. That's why so many of them are short-sighted. Quotas are also what Spanish journalists ask for.

R IS FOR RAILWAYS. The Europeans are very proud of their railways. France and Germany now have trains that go as fast as most jet planes, but then so do we. Though in our case, the planes are still on the ground. Being serviced. They may not be the fastest but at least we can boast that our trains run on grime. For all their speed and space-age technology, the European supertrains are strangely old-fashioned in some ways, hanging onto outmoded ideas we abandoned long ago. For instance, they still have restaurant cars that serve proper meals. (If you and your companion want an improper meal they're quite happy to bring it to your compartment.) European railways still call their passengers 'passengers', unlike British Rail who now call them 'customers'. 'Passenger' is a word that suggests being transported from one place to another whereas 'customer' suggests somebody standing at a counter waiting forever to be served. Ah, it begins to make sense.

European trains are still very romantic. When you're racing through the night on the Rhinemaiden Express, with only the lights of some distant schloss for company, it's still possible to imagine that some beautiful, mysterious female is about to burst into your compartment and beg to play Eve Marie Saint to your Cary Grant. Whereas on the 16.40 (Limited Buffet) Intercity to Bradford, the sexiest words you're likely to hear are 'You finished with that paper?'

On a more humdrum note, when you travel by train at least you know where your luggage is.

R is also for **REHOBOAM,** a wine bottle about one and a half times as big as a jeroboam which is about four times as big as a normal bottle. If your hotel offers a free bottle of wine with dinner ask for a rehoboam. You may not get it but they'll look at you with new respect.

R is also for **REICH,** which means the German Commonwealth. They've had three so far. If you start hearing the German people shouting 'Four' they may not be playing golf.

R is also for **RETSINA,** the only wine in the world that goes with Greek food. And you know where Greek food goes.

★

R is also for **RHINE,** the German river which nations have fought over for centuries and soon to be the subject of a new Channel 4 series, *Whose Rhine Is It Anyway?*

R is also for **ROGER,** which the Europeans regard as a proper noun and not a verb.

R is also for **ROGET,** who sounds French but was, in fact, English and who devised the Thesaurus, diction-

ary, word-list, lexicon, glossary, vocabulary, nomenclator, promptorium and wordhoard, for people who like a choice of words. Most Brits are happy with a few choice words.

***R is also for* ROME,** the Eternal City, the place to which all roads lead, except for the M11 which doesn't lead anywhere. Rome, which gave its name to the Treaty that started the whole shebang off in the first place, is where you do as the Romans do, that is, race round on scooters pinching women's bottoms and handbags, but not necessarily in that order. Anything goes in Rome, except the traffic. It was Roman decadence that inspired Fellini's $8\frac{1}{2}$, or $3\frac{1}{4}$ as it would have been in Iceland. One of Fellini's favourite actresses was Anita Ekberg, a magnificent creature who made Dolly Parton look anorexic; during the sixties, when they talked about the seven hills of Rome, two of them were Anita's.

The Colosseum in Rome is where they used to throw Christians to the lions, as opposed to the Coliseum in London where the ice-cream sellers do the reverse.

Rome is the home of the Vatican where His Holiness, the Pope, hands down his encyclicals to the faithful. (His most recent was *Encyclical Made For Two,* about married couples and the pill.) On his last visit to the United States the Pope attended a number of banquets in his honour, and being presented to His Holiness at one of these glittering affairs became the most important objective in many people's lives. At a dinner in Los Angeles attended by some of the most glamorous and elegant people in America, the Pope was proceeding along the receiving line when he came to a man who was wearing the filthiest, scruffiest dinner jacket imaginable, covered in crap and puke. To the amazement of everyone standing in that immaculate line the Pope leaned over and spoke to him. And the man nodded and walked away. Everybody thought: that's humility for you. All these beautifully dressed and important people but he only speaks to the one who looks like a bum. One of the men towards the end of the line raced after the bum. 'I'll give you ten thousand dollars for your jacket and I'll give you mine.' 'You crazy?' said the bum. 'Twenty thousand.' 'Done.' And, now wearing the vile jacket, he took his place back in the line, his heart beginning to pound as the Pope got closer and closer. Finally the Pope stood in front of him and sure enough he leaned over and spoke. 'I thought I told you to get the hell out of here.'

Rome is also where the Italian government stands. They would sit but they're never in power long enough.

R is also for **ROTTWEILER,** described by the dictionary as a tall German breed. So is Michael Stich but he doesn't go round biting the legs off your baby. Apparently Rottweilers are German hunting dogs, in which case we should use them for the purpose they were intended, hunting Germans.

R is also for **RUGBY,** which the French play rather well. Bastards.

R is also for **RULES AND REGULATIONS** (see Brussels, Common Market, EC, ERM, EMS, Eurocrats etc., etc., etc.).

★

R is also for **RUSSIA** which is not yet a member of the European Community but is thinking of begging for membership, which is ironic when you consider that a couple of years ago they could have taken their place at the big table in Brussels, and everybody else's as well. Gorbachev and Yeltsin, the Pinky and Perky of global politics, seem to be vying with each other to tear down the old Party structure and drag Russia into the twentieth century. There's talk of a Moscow Stock Exchange modelled on the London Stock Exchange and Gorbachev has already asked for a list of the phrases that are used most in the City of London, phrases like: 'Not guilty,' 'I'm appealing,' 'I shall repay every penny' and 'What are the visiting days at Ford Open Prison?'

Of course the jokes are now circulating about life in the new Russia. Gorbachev apparently disbands the KGB and they all take jobs as taxi drivers. When you get in you just give them your name. They know where you live. President Reagan had a favourite Russian joke. You do all remember President Reagan? Good. He doesn't. But this is his joke. A Russian got a phone call from his local garage. 'Good news, Yuri, I've got a delivery date for your new car.' 'When is it, Sergei?' '27 October 1996.' 'Morning or afternoon, Sergei?' 'What do you mean, Yuri, morning or afternoon? What difference does it make?' 'The plumber's coming that day.'

S IS FOR SADE, as in Marquis (pronounced marquee) de Sade, the French aristo who gave us the word 'sadism'. He was a man who certainly knew which side he liked his broad battered, and was very popular with his servants. Whenever he went out in his coach he insisted on having a whip round for the driver. The Marquis has always been popular with upper-class British pervs who were always putting him up in the garden.

Ask your travel agent about the new theme park opening near Paris next summer, Marquis de Sadeland. Everything's spanking new and they say the staff are unbeatable. The manager's usually tied up, which is a good sign, and the chambermaids, actually they're torture-chambermaids, would rather punch guests than pillows. It's the only place in France where 'pain' doesn't mean bread. Even the car rental Hertz. The theme park has its own restaurant chain which they shackle you to every mealtime, and all the meat's well hung. Don't worry if you're a vegetarian, they do exciting things with nuts. Sadeland has its own television station which transmits old Jeremy Beadle shows to all rooms twenty-four hours a day and it can't be switched off. Guests can't call room service, they have to go down on their knees and beg for what they want (not everything is different) and the hall porter not only makes new arrivals carry their own luggage but everybody else's as well. Some visitors are unsure what sort of tip they should leave. The top of a finger should be enough.

★

S is also for SCOTLAND or that bit to the north of England as some people call it. There are some who think that the Scots, inspired by events in Eastern Europe and Russia, want to break away and form a new state, and if they do it on a Saturday night we all know what state that will be.

Here are ten things you must never say to a Scotsman:

Hoots mon and och aye the noo.

Kenny Dalglish is a fairy.

See you, Jimmy.

Donald, where's your troosers?

What do you like about the English?

How about buying us a drink?

You'd be nothing without our oil.

Have you got any Irish whiskey?

What's the Gaelic for 'you drunken old fart'?

I'm your Conservative candidate.

S is also for **SERVICE** which is a word you don't hear much in Britain these days either in shops or the Church of England. About the only place you do hear it is on a tennis court and it's usually bloody awful there as well. With certain reservations (see Paris) the Europeans actually appear to enjoy serving you, which will come as something of a shock to people whose only means of getting a shop assistant's attention has been to take away her nail file. And you may also hear words that will shock you. Words like 'Can I help you?' 'I'll see if we've got it in stock' and 'Thank you for shopping with us.'

S is also for **SEX,** which the Europeans take for granted and we make jokes about. What do you do about sex? About sex we usually have our tea (trad. Scottish). What's the Englishman's idea of foreplay? Ready? The difference is summed up by two different plays that appeared on the London stage, *Sex Please We're Italian* and *No Sex Please, We're British*. *No Sex Please* was one of the longest running plays in British theatrical history and some were surprised that it didn't fold on the first night, as so many British husbands are supposed to do.

In what other country would a mother advise a nervous daughter to lie back and think of England? (In Wales they used to tell them to lie back and think of

Mike England, and it's rumoured that in her darkest Westland Helicopter days Mrs Thatcher used to lie back and think of Britten.) We frown upon the sexual peccadillos of our politicians, or, in the case of Norman 'He shot my dog' Scott, the peckapillows. Maurice Chevalier thanked heaven for little girls, we have social workers who thank heaven for little boys. Psychologists believe that the root of our dislike of the French stems from their sexual superiority. Frenchmen are the best lovers in the world and if you don't believe that, just ask them. They claim they give women what they want. In our experience what women want is alimony. Perhaps the French love of food has something to do with it. Perhaps we should note the way in which they linger over lunch and dinner. How they nibble their first course, get stuck into the main dish and then bring it all to a magnificent conclusion with a perfectly timed dessert. Our tempo is more McDonalds. 'To eat here or to go? Thank you for coming. Have a nice day.'

You can tell a lot about a nation's sex life from its cars. Only the French, for instance, would invent a car that rises every time you switch on the engine. And you can tell a lot about European women from the cars European men drive. (This is not chauvinist, cars don't have the same sexual significance for women as they do for men. To a woman a car's bonnet is not an extension of her sexuality. That's why a woman driver doesn't go crazy when some idiot cuts in front of her. To her it's just a near miss, to a man it's like having three inches lopped off his willie. There are exceptions to this rule. Just hope you never meet one.) The French like a soft ride with self-levelling suspension. The Germans like a firm ride and big models with huge bumpers that can go all day in the fast lane. The Italians like low-slung jobs that make a lot of noise when they take off. The Swedes like the lights on and one service a year. And the Brits like something from the company that they can fill up once a week. As we have suggested elsewhere, it can only be a matter of time before the EC get their hands on sex and then see how many people want to pull out.

S is also for **SKODA,** God's gift to gag writers. In fact there are probably more jokes about Skodas than there are Skodas. These are our favourites. What's the difference between a sheep and a Skoda? You don't feel ashamed being caught getting out of the back of a sheep. What do you call a bank robber who used a Skoda getaway car? The defendant. What do you get if you cross a Skoda with an MFI kitchen? A Lada with doors that won't close. What do you get if you cross a Skoda with an ambulance? A car with an invalid boot. How do you overtake a Skoda when it's going flat out? You just walk a bit faster.

S is also for **SPAIN.**
Ten things you must never say to a Spaniard:

    Gibraltar's British.

    I prefer Empire sherry.

    I'm with Club 18–30.

    Up the Basques.

If it wasn't for the Brits you'd still be riding donkeys.

My travel company's gone bust.

They're crap without Terry Venables.

What's the Spanish for 'wanker'?

What did you do under Franco?

Shame about the Armada.

★

S is also for SPERM-BANK. After 1992 you will be able to open accounts with any of the major European sperm-banks, including the Deutschwristbank, the Bank of Onan, Belgium's Thrustee Savings and the First Peppermill of Italy. Our advice would be to stick to established sperm-banks and ignore new outfits like BSSI, the Bank of Sperm and Stuff International, which collapsed, losing millions of deposits, when some private dick in America discovered it had been laundering sperm for the Mafia. Governments tend to wash their hands of this sort of thing.

★

S is also for SPONSORSHIP. This will increase in the New Europe as Japanese companies increasingly take over. Some financial analysts reckon that the Japanese buy-out will be complete by the year 2000 and entire countries will be sponsored. We'll be known as Mitsubishi Britain and we'll all be drinking Kawasaki French wine, eating Toshiba Belgian chocolates, wearing Sony Italian shoes and driving one car, the Honda Mercedes hatchback.

★

S is for SUPPOSITORIES. The bottom line is that French doctors believe that the cure for any ailment is a suppository. In fairness, we should point out they

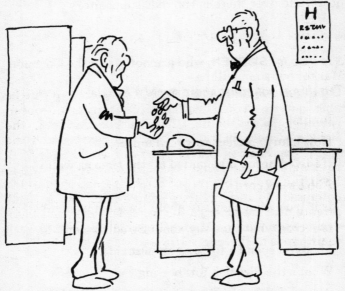

'I know you have an ear infection, but you stick them where I tell you to stick them!'

don't use the same suppository every time. An English visitor who had gone to a doctor complaining of some miner infection (something he'd picked up from Arthur Scargill) was given a handful of the lethal-looking bum bombs par le quaque. The Brit studied them for a few seconds and then said to the doctor: 'And I suppose you want me to stick these up my.....' 'Precisely, monsieur,' said the doctor.

Try not to confuse the words 'suppository' and 'depository'. A party of visiting French businessmen are still recovering from the shock of being told by one of their hosts 'and over there is Harrods suppository'.

★

S is also for SWEDEN, who are not yet in the Common Market but soon will be.
Ten things you must never say to a Swede:

Lights!

How many suicides in your family?

If I lived here I'd be pissed all the time as well.

Abba were crap.

Is it true what they say about Swedish women?

Is it true what they say about Swedish men?

I bet you spend a fortune on peroxide.

What's the Swedish for 'bor-ing'?

Say something in English, like 'aerosol'. Makes me fall about.

Don't jump.

Sweden is not the only country in line to join the Common Market. There's also Norway, Austria, Finland and Hungary. This will lead to some new definitions of Hell. Hell is where the wine waiter is Austrian, where the Samaritans are Swedish, where the song writers are Norwegian, where the second-hand car salesman is a Hungarian and where the barman is a Finn called Mickey.

S is also for SWITZERLAND.
Ten things you must never say to a Swiss:

Lend us a quid.

Apart from the cuckoo clock what else have you done?

My train was late.

What's wrong with Japanese watches?

These days they'd get William Tell for child abuse.

I like Belgian chocolate.

What did you do in the war, then?

What's the Swiss for 'tight bastards'?

Got much Colombian drug money in your bank?

I've forgotten my account.

T IS FOR TORREMOLINOS. Once described as Europe's largest open prison, Torremolinos is the spiritual home, the shrine at the end of the Watneys rainbow, for hundreds of thousands of Brits who make a yearly pilgrimage to this holy place. With Spain hosting the 1992 Olympics in Barcelona, Torremolinos has been chosen as the site for the Alternative Olympics. Birmingham had wanted to stage this event – they sent Edwina Currie to speak on their behalf but she laid an egg – and when the best location they could offer for the free style standing jump was three shop doorways in the Bullring, the International Committee opted for Spain.

A strong British contingent will compete and the Brits are expected to do well again in those events they have made their own; Throwing Up The Discus, the 5,000 Litres, Tossing The Locals, and Synchronized

Spewing. The main track event is the 400 Ritas which was won by the Italians in '88 in the staggering time of 26 hours and 43 minutes, (after 400 Ritas you'd be staggering), closely followed by the French who would have won if they hadn't kept stopping to get something to eat. In third place were the Greeks who came from behind at the last minute.

T is also for **TRABANT,** the East German car which makes your average Skoda look like a Ferrari. The Trabant is the only car in the world which gets queues of milk floats trying to overtake it. Most cars have a gear for overtaking, the Trabant has a gear for undertaking. If you want to double a Trabant's value top up the oil.

T is for **TURKEY,** another country who will want to join the Common Market.
Ten things you must never say to a Turk:

Give us a Greek coffee.

Have you seen *Midnight Express*?

Personally I prefer Fry's.

Some of my best friends are Kurds.

Got any Chinese carpets?

Why don't you just let them have Cyprus?

Miss, your moustache tickles.

What's the Turkish for 'I wouldn't fancy meeting you in an alley on a dark night, Mustapha'?

I'd rather have a sauna.

Know where I can get a copy of *Satanic Verses*?

***T is also for* TWIN TOWN,** which is something else that will probably vanish if the Europrats have their way. Just the term 'Twin Town' cries out for a whole new bunch of rules and regulations from Brussels. 'Unless two towns are identical in every regard, i.e., the same number of streets, the same size of population, the same number of pretty eighteen-year-olds with fantastically long legs and incredibly short skirts, the same number of McDonalds, the same number of vandalized telephones, the same number of dog turds on the pavements, etc., etc., then such towns may not call themselves "Twin Towns". Depending on the answers to the above they may call themselves "Nearly Alike Towns", "Quite Alike Towns" or "Absolutely Nothing Like Each Other Towns – But Still Quite Friendly".' Many of these towns must be coming up to the forty-fifth anniversary of their twinning and doubtless their civic dignitaries are on the look-out for a really spectacular way to celebrate the event. If you're twinned with a German town, say Hamburg or Dresden why not suggest reciprocal daylight bombing raids? But insist you have first go.

U IS FOR U-BOAT, the German submarines which caused the Allies a lot of hassle in World War II. For instance, whenever an Allied submarine got down to the seabed they found some German had stuck his towel on it.

★

U is also for **UMLAUT,** which is German for somebody who gets legless on pints of um.

★

U is also for the **URALS,** one of the great mountain ranges of Russia. Traditionally the Cossacks used to hang the peasants up by the Urals.

'I want to hang this damn peasant up by his Urals but he doesn't seem to have any.'

★

U is also for USHANT, which is a small island off the coast of Brittany and the noise the French make when they sneeze.

★

U is also for **UTOPIA,** which is presumably what the Eurocrats, and the Commissioners in Brussels believe they are creating in Europe. They might be better off leaving it to Disney.

V IS FOR VENICE where the strongest perfume is still Canal No 5. Venice is built on a foundation of tree trunks that were sunk into the ground hundreds of years ago. It's the only place in the world where the people are glad they've got piles. It's against the law in Venice to paddle in the canals (we did say paddle), and men can be fined for walking around bare-chested or in their bathing trunks or underpants. Women in bikinis get pinched as well. No visit to Venice is complete without somebody grabbing your cornetto, but don't retaliate unless you want to get caught by the gondoliers.

★

'Under arrest? What, me?'

V is for VIN, VINO AND VINHO which everybody thought would cost us, at most, about five pee a bottle after 1992. But there are suggestions that this isn't going to be the case, or even the half-case. It seems we could still be paying duty on that boot-load of booze from the hypermarket outside Boulogne. Write to your MP or to Oliver Reed or George Best to complain and get the law changed immediately. After all, cheap booze is the reason most of us wanted to go into Europe in the first place.

★

***V is for* VORSKIN DURCH TECHNIK,** a German condom which is very popular with young people who are looking for German reliability with Italian styling. It has the lowest drag factor in its class with a front end that crumples upon impact. It has a comfortable driving position, is good through the bends and enjoys being pushed to the limit. Nikki said it made him shout even louder. Voted European Condom Of The Year by *What Condom*.

W IS FOR WAR. Don't mention it.

★

W is for **WARSAW,** the capital of Poland, which is another country that's going to want to get into the Common Market.
Ten things you must never say to a Pole:

I prefer Russian vodka.

The Secret Police were only doing their job.

Got anything to eat?

Lech who?

I know you had Chopin and Lizst but have you ever heard Mrs Mills?

Would you like to hear a Polish joke?

I don't know what you people see in Margaret Thatcher.

What's the Polish for 'miserable bastard'?

But would you let your sister marry a Russian?

I can't stand your ham.

Mrs Thatcher is very popular with the Poles. If she'd been as popular with the polls she would still be in Downing Street. When she visited Poland the people used to get out on the streets and mob her, unlike Britain where the mob in the streets used to go out to get her. She used to have particular words of encouragement for Polish shipyard workers: 'We're closing down all the shipyards in Britain.'

It is ironic, is it not, that at the very time that we are embroiled in a great movement to create a united Europe, federations throughout Eastern Europe are splintering as individual countries start to reassert themselves and choose independence. Besides, life is so much more colourful when there are lots of different countries, especially for stamp collectors. But if the Eurocrats achieve their dream of one currency how do we know that it will stop there. Will it be one postal service with one set of stamps? (See Royalty. Will there be wars to decide whose head should be on them?) Will it be one cut of bacon? One shape of sausage? One potato crisp? One language even? It will no longer be *vive la différence* because there will be no bloody difference. Then the fun will start.

★

***W is also for* WEREWOLF.** Simple, superstitious peasant folk believed werewolves existed in Central Europe. At certain times of the month, people, helpless to avert the process, changed into crazed beasts who howled in the night and hunted down men and attacked them. These days we call it PMT.

'Oh my God, it's not that time of the month again already, is it?'

X IS A LETTER THAT IN EUROPE IS ONLY FOUND IN THE NAMES OF BELGIAN RACING CYCLISTS.

***X IS FOR* XENOPHOBE,** a person who hates foreigners, and for XENOPHILE, a person who likes foreigners. But when we're all one great big Eurostodge who will be the foreigners? We think the Chinese are in for a lot of stick.

★

'I've always been a xenophobe, but in your case I shall
make an exception.'

Y IS FOR YUGOSLAVIA. We're indebted to the *Daily Mail* for pointing out, with this story, that the Bosnians are the Irish of Yugoslavia. A Bosnian, wearing traditional peasant clothing, went into a shop in Belgrade to buy an accordion. The shopkeeper called him a stupid Bosnian peasant and threw him out. The next day the Bosnian went back to the shop and the same thing happened. He thought, I know what it is, it's these peasant clothes. So he put on a suit and tie and went back to the shop and again the shopkeeper called him a stupid Bosnian peasant and threw him out. He said, 'But I'm wearing ordinary clothes. How do you know I'm Bosnian?' And the shopkeeper said, 'Who else would try to buy an accordion in a shop that sells radiators?'

★

Z IS FOR ZURICH. (See EMS and Ken Dodd.)

Z is also for **ZZZZ**, which until now is what most Brits did when somebody started talking about Europe.

JIM HUTCHINGS.

'Is it the booze or did someone mention Europe?'